Make

Before appointing
hills and spent the   e

"The apostles, toge   **s**
prayer" (as they p   **y**
Spirit). Acts 1:14

If you desire to have a
living relationship with
Jesus, quality prayer time is
a must.

In fact, Jesus is calling you
to spend a certain amount of
time in prayer each day.

If you ask Him, He will
reveal to you what length of
time this is.

Thank You, Jesus, that You will help me to relax, to
be still and to sit at Your feet in prayer.

Help me to realise, Lord, that taking time to pray is
as important as taking time to eat or to rest.

Thank You, Jesus, that You will draw me into deep
union with Yourself as I pray, and that You will open
me to the full outpouring of the Holy Spirit.

(Pause and relax into Jesus who lives within you.)

1

Redeemed Sinners

The religious man marched up to the front of the temple and prayed, "Oh thank You, Lord for making me such a wonderful person." The sinner bowed his head and prayed, "Lord, be merciful to me a sinner." Luke 8:10

"We are justified by God's grace as a gift." Rom 3:23

Accept this free gift, and accept Jesus as your Saviour.

But always remember that you are a redeemed sinner; that it is by God's grace that you have been set free.

Lord Jesus, I come to You in sincere repentance for every sin I have ever committed. But I also come with total trust in Your mercy, accepting You as my Lord and Saviour.

Lord, bless every person into whose life I have ever brought hurt or disappointment, (especially ....)

And grant me the grace to be totally honest and frank in the Sacrament of Confession.

(Pause to hold this prayer in your heart before Jesus.)

A Heart Transplant

"I shall cleanse you to the depth of your being. I shall give you a new heart, and impart my Spirit to you. I shall remove your heart of stone, and give you a heart full of love. " Ezek 36:25-27

Jesus is not interested in us being just a bit more religious or saying a few more prayers.

He desires nothing less for us than a complete heart transplant; for us to be completely transformed from within, and for our hearts to be united with His heart.

Thank You, Jesus, that You are giving me this new heart.

Deliver me, Lord, from all hardness of heart.
Deliver me, Lord, from all selfishness of heart.
Deliver me, Lord, from all meanness of heart.
Deliver me, Lord, from all bitterness of heart.
Deliver me, Lord, from all impurity of heart.

Heal and cleanse my heart, Lord Jesus. Unite my heart with Your heart, and flood it with Your love.

(Pause. Mentally picture Jesus cleansing your heart.)

To Be Born Again

"Unless one is born again of water and the Holy Spirit one cannot be part of the Lord's kingdom." John 3:5

Nicodemus was a man of prayer. He was totally dedicated. But instead of complimenting him for all this, Jesus told him that he needed to be born again.

Up to then, his religion had come from his own efforts. "What is born of the flesh is flesh" John 3:6.

Now he needed to allow himself to be transformed from within by the power of the Holy Spirit. "What is born of the Spirit is spirit"

Lord Jesus, I desire the fullness of the rebirth. Flood my heart with Your love and with Your living presence.

O Holy Spirit penetrate every area of my being with Your healing, cleansing and delivering power. Deliver me from all selfishness and from every compulsion.

Lord Jesus, thank You that You have won for me the right to total personal transformation, including the complete healing and cleansing of my heart, my mind my emotions, my attitudes, and my sexuality.

(Invite the Holy Spirit to transform your inner being.)

Jesus In Your Heart

"**May God touch you in a mighty way in your inner self. May Jesus come alive in your heart as you learn to trust Him, and may He flood your entire being with love.**" Eph 3:16-18

When we receive Holy Communion the Sacred Host goes down into our tummies.

A great transfer needs to take place, so that as the Sacred Host goes down into our tummies, Jesus will come alive in our hearts.

Thank You, Jesus, that You are coming alive in my heart; that You are making Your home within me.

Grant me the grace of a total spiritual breakthrough, the full bursting forth of Your love in my heart.

Bring my inner being to life through Your presence. May the streams of living water well up within me.

(Pause. Mentally picture Jesus coming alive within you.)

Called To Become Jesus

"He or she who eats my flesh and drinks my blood lives in Me and I live in him or her." John 6:56

"We are to become the Body of Christ, His own flesh and blood." Pope Benedict (WYD 2005)

The first step is to have Jesus come alive in one's heart. But Jesus calls us to something far more radical:- to live in Him.

Our calling is nothing less than to become the living presence of Jesus in the world - to become His hands, His feet, His voice, His face, His heart, and His mind.

But to have "the mind of Christ", (1 Cor 2:16), we need "a complete make-over of our minds." Rom 12:2

Lord Jesus, transform my mind by the healing, cleansing and delivering power of the Holy Spirit.

Lord, help me to spot and to renounce every thought that does not come from You.

Lord Jesus, teach me how to become Your mind, Your hands, Your feet, Your eyes, Your ears, Your face, and Your voice in today's world.

(Pause. Invite the Holy Spirit to transform your mind.)

Surrendering One's Ambitions

"Unless you change and become like little children, you will not be part of my kingdom. The one who humbles himself like a little child is the greatest in the kingdom of heaven." Mt. 18:3-4

In the early stages of the spiritual life, it is normal to have the ambition to achieve, the ambition to be recognised, and the ambition to be a success in human terms.

But if we are to be the living presence of Jesus in the world, all these ambitions need to be surrendered to Jesus.

Lord Jesus, I renounce all self-seeking ambition, and all divisive ambition.
I renounce the desire to be recognised as important, and the desire to be seen to be influential.
Lord, I entrust all my ambitions to You.

My one ambition now is to become
Your voice, Your hands, Your face;
To live in total union with You;
And to help my loved ones to do the same.

(Pause, desiring total union with Jesus and His will.)

To Pray With Voice of Jesus

"If you abide in Me, I will abide in you. Then you will bear much fruit . ... I will begin to prompt you, and your prayers will be answered again and again."
John 15: 5b, 7

Before Jesus cried over Jerusalem, you can be sure that He prayed long and hard for its conversion. Prayer wins opportunities for people, but they can still reject those opportunities.

Yet Jesus saw mighty answers to prayer, and so too can we - if we learn to live in Him, and to pray with His voice.

Lord Jesus,
May my thoughts spring from Your thoughts;
May my prayers spring from Your prayers;
May it no longer be I who pray,
But You Lord, who prays through me.

May my heart be united with Your heart;
May my faith be energised by Your faith;
And may I see powerful answers to prayer.

(Pause. Invite Jesus to pray through you.)

8

Renounce Judgementalism

"Do not judge and you will not be judged." Luke 6:37

"Why do you see the speck in your brother's eye and do not see the beam in your own eye?" Mt. 7:3

To have the mind of Jesus and to pray with His voice, one must renounce judgementalism and all unloving thoughts and seek to be delivered from them.

Judgementalism is a symptom that there is anger and insecurity in one's own heart that needs to be dealt with.

Deliver me, Lord, from the spirit of judgementalism.
Deliver me, Lord, from all inner anger and insecurity.
Deliver me, Lord, from jumping to false conclusions.
Deliver me, Lord, from all un-Godly thoughts.
Deliver me, Lord, from all evil spirits (especially ......)

Thank You, Jesus, that You will enable me to see
other people through Your eyes,
And to love them with Your love for them.

(Pause. Unite yourself with the love of Jesus who is within you.)
(To offer this prayer for someone else, just replace "me"
with the person's Christian name.)

One's Suffering

"In my flesh, I complete what is lacking in Christ's afflictions for the sake of His body, that is the Church."
Col 1:24

When we live in Jesus and He in us, our entire being, including our sufferings become united with Jesus living within us.

Our sufferings, including tiredness and inner anguish, then become an extension of His redemptive suffering.

It is, however, the risen Jesus who lives within us, so even as we offer up our sufferings in union with His sufferings, we pray also to be touched by the power of His resurrection.

Lord Jesus, I surrender myself and all my sufferings to You who are living within me.

Sanctify my sufferings, Lord Jesus. May blessing be released through them, (especially for ....)

But I also pray, Lord, to be touched by the power of Your resurrection:- to be lifted up, to be given strength, and to experience your healing love.

(Become conscious of Jesus within you. Then surrender your sufferings to Him, and draw strength from Him.)

Being The Hands Of Jesus

"Since you were faithful in small things, I will put you in charge of large matters." Luke 19:17

Jesus spent some thirty years doing the ordinary things.

We are called to be the hands of Jesus and the feet of Jesus in everything we do - even when washing dishes or sweeping the floor.

Often we desire to do something big or exciting immediately, but normally we must first mature while being faithful in little things.

Lord, help me to realise that in my daily work, my hands can be Your hands and my feet Your feet.

May I do my daily work in deep union with You, Lord, and under Your anointing. May I make all the right choices, and take all things in my stride.

Grant me a special appreciation for those who spend their lives doing the more menial tasks. To them, Lord, may I be Your face, Your ears and Your voice.

(Pause and become conscious of how your hands can become the hands of Jesus in your everyday work)

"Tell Your Family"

Jesus told the man who had been delivered, "Return to your home and tell your family how much God has done for you." Luke 8:39

If you love Jesus, you will thirst for the day when each member of your family will have come to a living relationship with Him.

You will have a vision of Jesus being Lord of your home.

And you will long for Him to be Lord of the homes of your children and your children's children.

Lord Jesus, I invite You to consecrate my home and family to Your Sacred Heart.

May each member of my family come to a living relationship with You and establish You as Lord of their homes.
I ask especially for ..... (& ..... &......)
Immerse ..... in the rays of your mercy.

Lord, teach me how to become Your living presence to my family.

(Mentally picture Jesus blessing key family members.)

The Eucharist

"This is My body which will be given up for you. ... This is My blood which will be offered for you ... Do this is memory of Me." (See Lk 22:20)

Did you realise that in Mass we are called to offer our own lives in union with Jesus to the eternal Father?

Only then do we fulfil the command, "Do this in memory of Me."

Lord Jesus, in each Mass,
Help me to offer my body along with Your body;
To offer my blood along with Your blood;
To offer my life along with Your life.

(Pause and unite yourself with Jesus' self-offering to the Father.)

Lord Jesus, as I unite myself with You each time in Mass, I pray that your blessings will be poured out upon ... (Write your intentions here)

....

....

Television and Papers

"Don't let the world determine how you think, but let God be the one who moulds your thinking." Rom 12:1

"If your eye causes you to sin, pluck it out." Mk 9:47

Television can be a wonderful gift, but it can also be a source of great corruption. The same is true of both the internet and newspapers.

Invite Jesus to become Lord of your TV, your computers and of what you read.

Lord Jesus, I consecrate my television, my computer and my newspapers to you.

Lord, I pray for the grace to only watch and read what You and I, Lord, can watch and read together.

Grant my family the grace, Lord, to reject all the works of the evil one in the media.

(Especially protect .... from all evil in ....).

I also pray, Lord, for the raising up of dynamic Christian television and radio in our country.

(Pause to hold this prayer in your heart before Jesus)

Heroic Love

"Father, as You are in Me, and I am in You, may they so live in us, that the world will recognise that it was You who sent me." John 17:21

If your heart is to be united with the heart of Jesus, then it needs to learn to love with the love of Jesus.

This isn't possible in human terms, but it is possible by the power of the Holy Spirit. Think of someone you find it hard to love. Become conscious of Jesus' love for h... Then unite yourself with His love for h...

Lord Jesus, help me to surrender all my hurts and all my anger to You, and to become united with You in Your love for even the worst sinners.

Whatever mistakes people have made, whatever problems they now have, whatever hurt they have caused, grant me the grace to still love them.

Grant me the grace, Lord, to become the living embodiment of Your love, especially to my family.

(Become aware of the infinite love of Jesus who is within you. Invite it to flow through your very veins.)

15

Jesus, I Trust In You

"Commit your cause to the Lord, trust in Him and he will act on your behalf." Ps. 37:5

Jesus told St. Faustina, "The graces of my mercy are drawn by means of one vessel only, and that is - trust.

"The more a soul trusts, the more it will receive.

"Souls that trust boundlessly are a great comfort to me, because I pour all the treasures of my graces into them." Diary 1578

Deliver me, Lord, from the spirit of worry.
Deliver me, Lord, from the spirit of mental agitation.
Deliver me, Lord, from the spirit of fear.
Deliver me, Lord, from the spirit of anxiety.

Lord Jesus, I entrust every situation to You, especially ....

Lord, for the grace to really trust You,
The grace to trust that Your way is always best,
The grace to know that You will never let me down.

(Pause and entrust your whole life to Jesus)

To Be Guided By You, Lord

"The Lord desires to guide you always and He will satisfy your desire for what is right." Isaiah 58:11

"The Lord leads the humble into His plan for their lives." Ps. 25:9

We are not pure spirits. We will never be able to perfectly hear God in every situation, so prayer for guidance needs to be approached with real humility.

Yet, if we seek His guidance with humility and trust, then Jesus will guide us.

**Lord Jesus, I do desire to hear your voice.
I do desire to be guided by You in all things.**

Lord, if I am ever stepping outside Your plan for my life, block me. Put obstacles in my path.

Likewise if I am slow in responding to Your call, do something to stir me up, Lord.

O Holy Spirit, make me sensitive to Your guidance in every situation.

Thank You that You desire to lead me into the fullness of Your special plan for my life.

(Invite Jesus to guide you. Listen. Perhaps open your Bible **ONCE** if praying about a particular situation.)

"Do You Love Me?"

A third time, Jesus asked, "Simon, son of John, do you love me?" Peter was upset that He asked him the third time, and replied, "Lord, You know all things. You know I love You." Jesus replied, "Feed my sheep." Jn 22:17

In asking Peter the three times, "Do you love Me?" Jesus was putting down a marker:- if we really love Him, then we will seek to feed His sheep.

"Anyone who has discovered Christ must lead others to Him." Pope Benedict

"Once I have Jesus, I have to bring Him to others." Blessed Mother Teresa

Lord, grant that I may never miss an opportunity to help another person in their spiritual journey.

May I never be held back by my shyness or lack of courage. Empower me, Lord, with the outpouring of the Holy Spirit.

Put a new courage into my heart. Put the right words on my lips. Inspire me to give the right gifts.

And give me a passion for leading people to You.

(Pause. Ask Jesus for practical guidance.)

Heroic Forgiveness

"Forgive us our sins as we forgive everyone who sins against us." Luke 11:4

"When you forgive those who sin against you, it opens you to the forgiving love of your heavenly Father."
Mt 6:14

Praying with the heart and voice of Jesus, requires heroic forgiveness.

This isn't to suggest that God doesn't love you if there is hurt in your life, or that you won't often see your prayers answered.

But if we are to pray with the voice of Jesus, then we need to forgive with the forgiveness of Jesus.

Lord Jesus, in faith, I now decide to forgive completely and totally every person who has ever hurt me or who ever will hurt me, including ......

Help me to take the right steps to come into this level of forgiveness, and the right steps to act out this type of unconditional forgiveness.

(Pause and unite yourself with the forgiveness of Jesus)

Heroic Thanksgiving

"Even if the whole world is collapsing, I will rejoice in God, and exult in the Lord my Saviour." Hab 3:16-17

"Rejoice in the Lord in every situation. Again I say, Rejoice." Phil 4:4

You don't have to thank God that someone is an alcoholic, but if you desire to pray with the voice of Jesus, then you do need to start thanking God for the person who is the alcoholic - and for God's love.

There are, of course, times for grieving, and times for working through one's emotions, but to see mighty answers to prayer, the spirit of praise and thanksgiving is necessary.

Lord Jesus, thank You that you will bring good for me out of every bad thing that has ever happened to me or ever will happen to me.

Thank You, Lord, that You are with me in every situation; and that in You, there is the answer to every problem.

With Mary I pray, "My soul glorifies the Lord, my spirit rejoices in God my Saviour." (Luke 1:46-47)

(Pause and let thanksgiving well up within you.)

Praying For Deliverance

"Put on all God's armour, for it isn't just flesh and blood we fight, but a whole host of evil spirits." Eph 6:11-12

Evil spirits are like viruses. Wherever one has a weak spot, they will infect. This is a not possession, but it intensifies our compulsion. We then need deliverance.

Where there is a severe problem, there will be several different spirits - for example behind the spirit of alcoholism, there will often be the spirits of self-deception, despair, manipulation, anger etc., etc.

When praying, we are not concerned as to where the human spirit ends and the evil spirit enters in. If a person is bitter, we pray for deliverance from the spirit of bitterness, without the need to distinguish between the human spirit of bitterness and the evil spirit which latches on to it.

Lord Jesus, I renounce all evil spirits.
Help me to recognise where they are at work,
and to become Your voice in praying for deliverance
from them.

Grant me, Lord, the gifts of discernment, right
judgement and prudence plus total faith in Your
power over all evil spirits.

(Pause and thank Jesus that in Him we have victory.)

For One In Spiritual Rebellion

Lord I forgive ..... completely and totally for every way (s)he has ever hurt me or ever will hurt me.

I thank you for .... including for h.. personality which challenges us to a strong love.

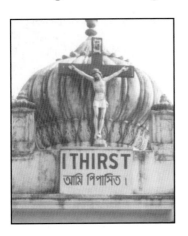

Pause to become aware of ...... as a real living human being with feelings and emotions.

Become conscious of Jesus' desire to lead .... to a living relationship with Himself.

Then with love in your heart, and pausing after each line, pray,

Lord, deliver .... from the spirit of rebellion.
Deliver ...... Lord, from the spirit of anger.
Deliver ...... Lord, from spiritual darkness.
Deliver ...... Lord, from all evil spirits
(including the spirit of .... and the spirit of ....)

Open ....'s heart and mind, Lord Jesus.
Somehow bring h.. to a living relationship with You.

(Pause. Hold .... before Jesus, with longing in your heart.)

For One Who Is Depressed

Lord I forgive ..... completely and totally for every way (s)he has ever hurt me or ever will hurt me.

I thank you for .... including for h.. personality which challenges us to a strong love.

Pause to become aware of ...... as a real living human being with feelings and emotions. Become conscious that for .... life is a real struggle.

Become conscious of Jesus' great love for .... and His desire to set h.. free. Unite yourself with this love.

Then with love in your heart, and pausing after each line, pray,

Lord, deliver ...... from the spirit of depression.
Deliver ...... Lord, from the spirit of despair.
Deliver ...... Lord, from the spirit of fear and anxiety.
Deliver ...... Lord, from the spirit of insecurity.
Deliver ...... Lord, from the spirit of self-hatred.
Deliver ...... Lord from all evil spirits
(including the spirit of .... and the spirit of ....)

Lord, grant .... the grace to trust You,
The grace to start drawing strength from You,
The grace to know that with Your help, (s)he can get on with the simple things of daily life,
And the grace to receive the best possible help.

(Pause. Hold .... before Jesus, with longing in your heart.)

For An Alcoholic or Addict

**Lord I forgive ..... completely and totally for every way
(s)he has ever hurt me or ever will hurt me.
I thank you for ....., including for h.. personality which
challenges us to a strong love.**

Pause to become aware of ...... as
a real living human being with
feelings and emotions.

Become conscious of Jesus' great
love for .... and His desire to set
..... free. Unite yourself with this
love.

Then with love in your heart, and
pausing after each line, pray,

Deliver ...... Lord, from the spirit of alcoholism.
(**OR** from the spirit of drug addiction).
Deliver ...... Lord, from the spirit of denial.
Deliver ...... Lord, from the spirit of bitterness.
Deliver ...... Lord, from the spirit of dependency.
Deliver ...... Lord, from the spirit of manipulation.
Deliver ...... Lord, from all evil spirits,
(including the spirit of .... and the spirit of ....)

**Lord, grant ... the grace to turn to You,
The grace to want to be delivered,
The grace to trust in Your power to set h... free,
The grace to seek the help (s)he needs.**
(Pause. Hold .... before Jesus, with longing in your heart.)

Where There Is Division

Lord I forgive ..... & ..... (& ....) completely and totally for any way they have ever hurt me or ever will hurt me.   I thank you for them, and that You love them as they are.

Pause to become aware of ......
& ..... (& ......) as real living
human beings with feelings and
emotions.

Become conscious of Jesus'
great love for them. Unite
yourself with this love.

Then with love in your heart,
and pausing after each line, pray,

Lord, deliver .... & .... (&...) from the spirit of bitterness.
Deliver them, Lord, from the spirit of abusiveness.
Deliver them, Lord, from the spirit of recrimination.
Deliver them, Lord, from the spirit of anger.
Deliver them, Lord, from the spirit of domination.

Deliver them, Lord, from all evil spirits
(including the spirit of .... and the spirit of ....)

**Lord, grant .... & .... (&...) the grace to know that
there is a better way to live.**
Lord, teach them the meaning of true love.
Lord, teach them to turn to You and to trust You.

(Hold ... & .... before Jesus, with longing in your heart.)

For One Who Is Separated

Lord I forgive ..... completely and totally for any way (s)he have ever hurt me or ever will hurt me.

I thank you for ...., and that You love .... as (s)he is.

Pause to become aware of ...... as a real living human being with feelings and emotions who may now be hurting deeply.

Become conscious of Jesus' great love for ..... Unite yourself with this love.   Then pausing after each line, pray,

Lord, grant .... the grace to surrender h.. life to You, and to trust You for the future.
Lord, heal all ....'s emotional wounds.

Deliver ..... Lord, from the spirit of hurt.
Deliver ..... Lord, from the spirit of bitterness.
Deliver ..... Lord, from the spirit of embarrassment.
Deliver ..... Lord, from the spirit of isolation.
Deliver ..... Lord from all sexual spirits, (especially ....)
Deliver ..... Lord, from all evil spirits, (especially ....)

Lord, draw ..... into Your loving embrace.
Protect h.. from all harm.
Fill h.. with Your strength.

(Pause. Hold .... before Jesus, with longing in your heart.)

For One Suffering Anorexia

Lord I forgive ..... completely and totally for every way (s)he has ever hurt me or ever will hurt me.
I thank you for ....., including for h.. personality which challenges us to deeper levels of love.

Pause to become aware of ...... as a real living human being with feelings and emotions.

Become conscious of Jesus' great love for .... and His desire to set h.. free. Unite yourself with this love.

Then with love in your heart, and pausing after each line, pray,

Lord Jesus, deliver .... from the spirit of anorexia.
Deliver ..... Lord, from the spirit of self hatred.
Deliver ..... Lord, from the spirit of denial,
Deliver ..... Lord, from the spirit of manipulation.
Deliver ..... Lord, from all evil spirits
(including the spirit of .... and the spirit of ....)

Fill ....'s heart with Your love.
Give h.. the desire to be healed.
Help h.. to trust You for transformation.
Bring h.. inner being back to life.
Come alive within h..., Lord Jesus.

(Pause. Hold .... before Jesus, with longing in your heart.)

27

For One Who Is Suicidal

Lord I forgive ..... completely and totally for every way (s)he has ever hurt me or ever will hurt me.

I thank you for ....., including for h.. personality which challenges us to deeper levels of love.

Pause to become aware of ...... as a real living human being with feelings and emotions.

Become conscious of Jesus' great love for .... and His desire to set h.. free. Unite yourself with this love.

Then with love in your heart, and pausing after each line, pray

Deliver ..... Lord, from the spirit of suicide.
Deliver ..... Lord, from the spirit of despair.
Deliver ..... Lord, from the spirit of desolation.
Deliver ..... Lord, from the spirit of isolation
Deliver ..... Lord, from the spirit of distrust in You.
Deliver ..... Lord from all evil spirits
(including the spirit of .... and the spirit of ....)

Lord, fill .....'s heart with Your love.
Help h.. trust You for the future.
Bring joy and hope into h.. life.
Protect h.. from all evil.
(Pause. Hold .... before Jesus, with longing in your heart.)

For One Who Is Bitter

Lord I forgive ..... completely and totally for every way (s)he has ever hurt me or ever will hurt me.

I thank you for ..... , including for h.. personality which challenges us to deeper levels of love.

Pause to become aware of ...... as a real human being with feelings and emotions, who has perhaps suffered real hurt and disappointments in life.

Become conscious of Jesus' great love for .... and His desire to set h.. free. Unite yourself with this love.

Then with love in your heart, and pausing after each line, pray

Deliver ..... Lord, from the spirit of bitterness.
Deliver ..... Lord, from the spirit of revenge.
Deliver ..... Lord, from the spirit of hatred.
Deliver ..... Lord, from spiritual blindness.
Deliver ..... . Lord from all evil spirits
(including the spirit of .... and the spirit of ....)

Lord, draw ..... into an experience of Your love.
Help h.. to take the steps that lead to healing.
**Help h.. to surrender everything to You
and to trust You.**

(Pause. Hold .... before Jesus, with longing in your heart.)

For One With Sexual Problems

Lord I forgive ..... completely and totally for every way (s)he has ever hurt me or ever will hurt me.

I thank you for ...., including for h.. personality which challenges us to deeper levels of love.

Pause to become aware of ...... as a real living human being with feelings and emotions, who has perhaps suffered real hurt and disappointments in life.

Become conscious of Jesus' great love for .... and His desire to set h.. free. Unite yourself with this love.

Then with love in your heart, and pausing after each line, pray

Deliver .... Lord, from the spirit of sexual selfishness.
Deliver .... Lord, from the spirit of pornography.
Deliver .... Lord, from the spirit of sexual fantasising.
Deliver .... Lord, from the spirit of denial.
Deliver .... Lord, from the spirit of manipulation.
Deliver .... Lord, from all sexual spirits especially .....
Deliver .... Lord, from all evil spirits
(including the spirit of .... and the spirit of ....)

Help ...... to recognise the destruction that sexual sins cause, and to accept You as Lord and Saviour. Draw h.. to Yourself, Lord Jesus.

(Pause. Hold .... before Jesus, with longing in your heart.)

Protection On The Roads

"As we travelled the road to Jerusalem, the hand of the Lord protected us from accidents, bandits, and from dangerous fellow travellers." Ezra 8:31

Living in Jesus has major implications for how one drives.

Here too we are called to be his Hands, His heart, His mind, His eyes, His ears and His feet.

We also need God's protection because some drivers leave themselves open to being used by evil spirits, while sometimes, evil spirits can take advantage of any defect in road or car or even a moment's distraction by the driver.

Lord, teach me how to be Your hands, Your feet, Your eyes, Your heart and Your mind when driving.

Deliver me from any spirit that could affect my driving, especially the spirit of ..... (and the spirit of ...)

I entrust my car to You. Send Your angels to watch over it. Protect us on the roads from all serious accidents and from all evil.

(Mentally picture yourself being Jesus' hands when driving.)

To offer this prayer for someone else just replace "me" with that person's name, etc.

For This Day, Lord

"It is no longer I who live, but Christ who lives in me. This union with Jesus, I live by ongoing faith." Gal 2:20

"We are being transformed from one degree of likeness to Jesus to another." 2 Cor 3:18

You are called to become the living presence of Jesus, to become His very body and blood.

Don't be frightened. Just relax into Jesus who is within you.

With total trust in Jesus, ask His help to enable you to stand in His place moment by moment for this day.

**Lord for this day,
May my heart be Your heart,
May my thoughts be Your thoughts,
May my hands be Your hands,
May my feet be Your feet,
May my eyes be Your eyes,
May my ears be Your ears,
May my voice be Your voice,
And may my face be Your face.**

(Now relax, and allow the presence of Jesus within you to flow through you.)
(Repeat all or part of this prayer regularly during the day.)